This Notebook Belongs To

____

Printed in Great Britain
by Amazon

71065165R00072